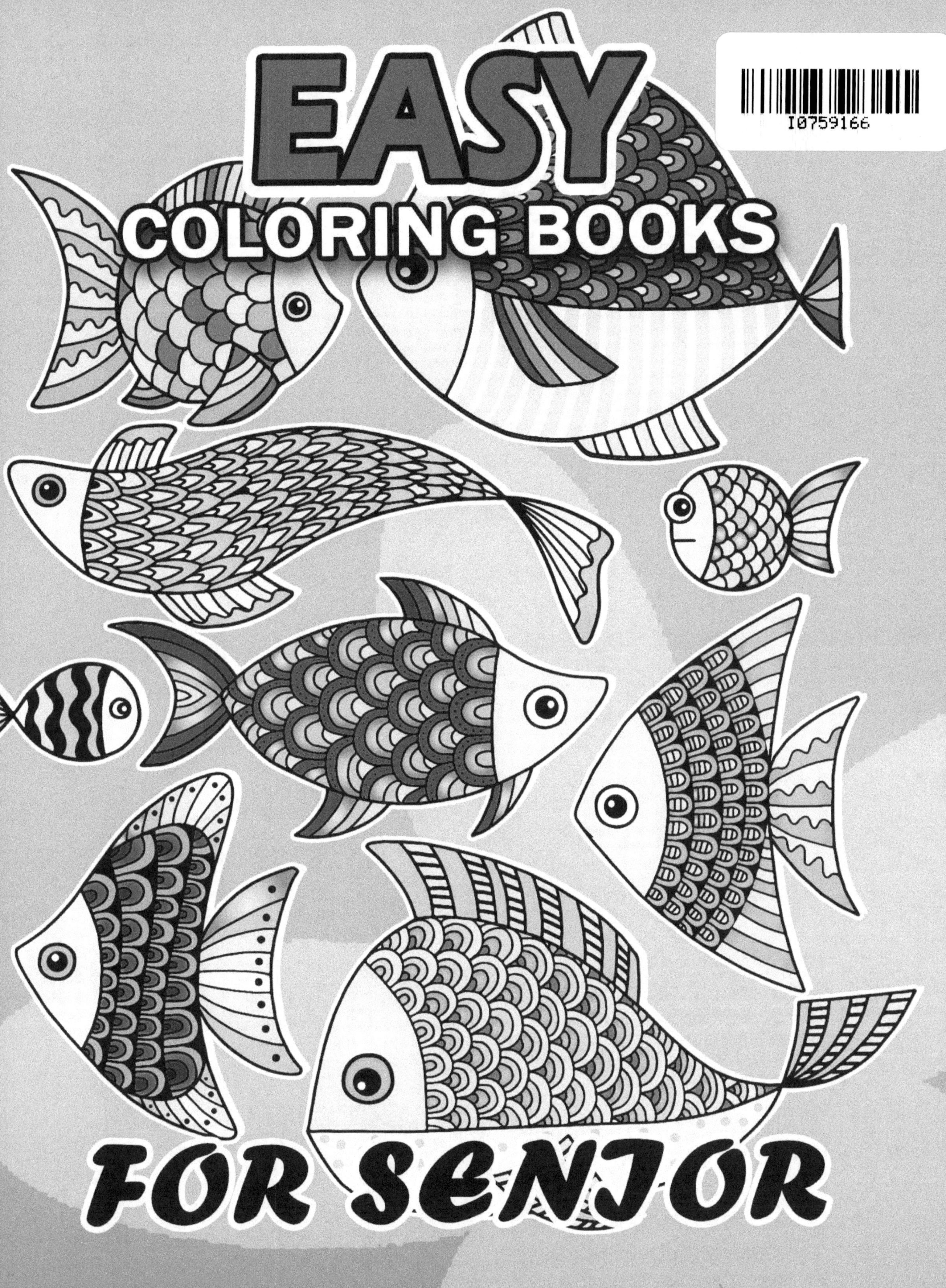

EASY
COLORING BOOKS
FOR SENIOR
I0759166

PUBLISHED IN 2018 BY
KODOMO PUBLISHING

PRINTED IN THE UNITED STATES OF AMERICA

COLOR TEST PAGE

Love

Love forever

I LOVE
TEA

Love forever

Happy
Family

Love

Love forever

I LOVE
TEA

Love forever

Happy
Family

www.ingramcontent.com/pod-product-compliance
Lightning Source LLC
Chambersburg PA
CBHW081842250726
48659CB00008B/2564